HUMAN RIGHTS

© Aladdin Books Ltd 1987

Designed and produced by
Aladdin Books Ltd
70 Old Compton Street
London W1

Library of Congress Catalog
Card Number: 87-80448

*First published in the
United States in 1987 by*
Gloucester Press
387 Park Avenue South
New York, NY 10016

Printed in Belgium

ISBN 0-531-17055-1

Editor: Catherine Bradley
Designer: Rob Hillier

*The author, Dr John Bradley, is an expert in international relations
and human rights. In 1975 he took part in a commission of enquiry
into human rights abuses during the Second World War. He taught
politics and international relations at the University of Manchester,
U.K., and is now teaching at the University of Bordeaux, France.*

*The consultant, Dr John Pimlott, is Senior Lecturer in war studies and
international affairs at the Royal Military Academy, Sandhurst, U.K.
He has written extensively on conflict in the 20th century.*

Contents

HUMAN RIGHTS

DR JOHN BRADLEY

Illustrated by

Ron Hayward Associates

Gloucester Press
New York : London : Toronto : Sydney

Human rights

At the April 1987 talks between the Soviet leader, Mikhail Gorbachev, and British prime minister, Margaret Thatcher, human rights was at the top of the agenda. But both leaders had different ideas as to what human rights meant.

Human rights make it possible for everyone to live as human beings. Over the centuries people have developed their ideas about human rights and what they mean, and many have died in the struggle to achieve them.

North America and Western Europe basically agree about what is meant by human rights. Human rights are generally divided into two types: civil and political rights, which cover the right to choose how one's country is run and to conduct one's life free from interference; and social, economic and cultural rights, which are concerned with the quality of life and having a decent standard of living.

Throughout the world many people are denied their rights. This book explains why this is happening in certain countries. It concentrates on major abuses of civil and political rights and why they occur. It also highlights the fact that for many the biggest obstacle to achieving human rights is poverty: they are so poor they can barely survive.

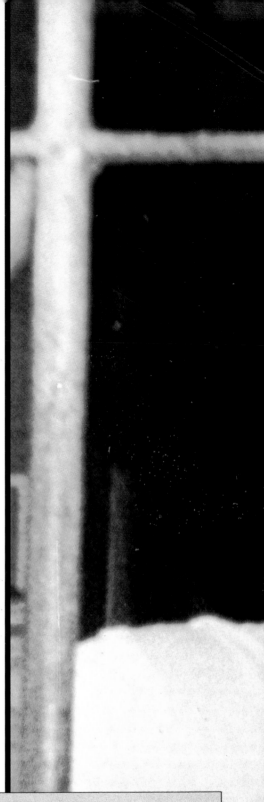

Social, economic and cultural rights
- the right to enough food, clothing, medical care, welfare or social security, education and housing
- the right to enjoy the culture of one's people

Civil and political rights
- the right to choose how a country is run
- no wrongful arrest
- the right to a fair trial
- the right to own property
- the right to work
- the right to freedom of thought and religion
- the right to leave and return to any country
- the right to freedom of opinion and expression
- the right to hold meetings
- the right to join groups
- the right to life
- freedom from slavery

One of the many thousands of political prisoners held in the Philippines. Political prisoners are usually imprisoned because they oppose the way their country is run.

Equal human rights?

Human rights are based on the idea that human beings are all equal and deserve fair and like treatment. It is an idea that has taken centuries to be accepted and not everyone agrees with it. Ideas about equality first arose in the early religious teachings of Judaism and Buddhism. These stressed the equality of all human beings before God or gods.

The Christian religion added freedom – because God was the final judge, people should be allowed to do as they wanted as long as it did not interfere with other people's rights. Laws were introduced to make sure that these rights were respected by everyone.

INEQUALITY

Some people think they are superior because they have more money, ability, power or racial superiority.

REPRESSION

The dominating group restricts rights: opposition is not allowed, torture is used by police, etc.

PREJUDICE

A group of people protect their power by thinking another group, usually a "minority," is inferior.

PROTEST

The "oppressed" protest peacefully in demonstrations, or violently with armed action.

OPPRESSION

One group dominates all others. The "oppressed" have less rights than those who dominate or are in power.

DISCRIMINATION

The "inferior" group cannot get jobs or housing. Women and Blacks often suffer from this.

However, it was in the 18th century that the ideas now held about human rights were mainly developed. They were laid down in documents such as the American Declaration of Independence in 1776 which stated that man's basic rights were "life, liberty and the pursuit of happiness." The French Revolution of 1789 got rid of many old privileges and laid down the right to vote.

In the 20th century, after two world wars (1914-18 and 1939-45), most countries of the world united in stating their support for human rights and their determination to avoid war. In 1948 the Universal Declaration of Human Rights was adopted by the United Nations (UN), the body representing most of the world's countries. This contained 30 Articles which stated how people and countries should treat each other by respecting "the equal rights of men and women and of nations large and small." After centuries of gradual progress, it seemed that human rights were accepted by all the peoples of the world.

Article 1. All human beings are born free and equal in dignity and rights. They are endowed with reason and conscience and should act towards one another in a spirit of brotherhood.

Universal Declaration of Human Rights

◁ Although human rights are based on the idea of equality, not everyone believes in this. Often this leads to a vicious circle, where everyone's rights are interfered with.

▽ The symbol of the United Nations.

Freedom...

It has taken some two thousand years to develop and establish democracy, in which the people can influence the running of a country, usually by electing a government. Fifth century Athens was the "cradle" of civilization. It had a system called direct democracy. Every adult citizen could join in discussions in the market place and vote to pass a law which would apply to all. However, those who were not citizens had no rights. Since this included slaves and women, the system was very limited.

Today most democratic systems hold elections every few years. If the people do not like the way their government is running the country they can get rid of it. Most elections are conducted peacefully but sometimes there is violence as rival groups try to make sure they win. For example, in the 1987 elections in the Philippines 80 people died. This compares well with the 100s who died in previous elections.

△ Martin Luther King Jr. leads a civil rights protest march in 1961. Black people in the United States have a history of being denied rights. Discrimination was rife in the South, where most of the Blacks lived. In the 1950s and 1960s Blacks organized in the civil rights movement. In 1964 a law, The Civil Rights Act, was passed, which was designed to end discrimination against Blacks over jobs and housing. Despite this act discrimination still exists.

△ A rally for the reelection of President Ronald Reagan.

...and democracy

Most democratic systems are based on constitutions, or sets of basic laws. In the United States the system consists of three separate parts: the executive (led by the President) runs the country; the legislative (the Congress) passes the laws and watches over the executive; and the judiciary (the judges and courts) interprets laws. Each part acts as a check on the other parts and thus protects the interests of the people. Every four years there are elections to choose a president. In President Lincoln's words democracy is a government "of the people, by the people and for the people."

Each democratic system is different. Some countries have no written constitution, for example, Britain and Israel. But they have laws that protect human rights. On the whole the democratic system is the best one for allowing human rights, because people can criticize their government. However it is not perfect.

PRESIDENT

"executes" government program and oversees foreign affairs. Can veto (reject) any law.

CABINET

a group of advisers who carry out policy and manage defense, foreign affairs, etc.

CONGRESS

passes new laws. Can reject President's proposals. It is made up of the following:

Senate

checks laws passed by the House of Representatives. Every state elects two Senators.

House of Representatives

checks laws passed by Senate. Total of 435 Representatives.

SUPREME COURT

consists of judges chosen by the President, approved by the Senate. Decides what a law means.

△ The American democratic system works because each part tries to check the others.

9

Freedom in the Soviet Union

The Soviet Union's record on human rights is poor. Throughout its history, the Russian Empire has had to protect its people from invasions, both from outside groups and from wandering nomads within its borders. Therefore security was more important than freedom.

In 1917, following the Russian Revolution, the Russian Empire became the Soviet Union. It developed a communist system of government, which was exported to Eastern Europe after 1945. This system gives great power to the Communist Party (CP), which is made up of 18 million out of 279 million citizens. The party runs the country. The state owns industry, agriculture and housing.

▽ Mikhail Gorbachev, General Secretary of the Communist Party, (seated far right, in front) attends a meeting of the Supreme Soviet.

POLITBURO

is a committee of 10 or 15 members, which heads the CP. It controls the CP by making all appointments to CP posts. Its chairman is the General Secretary, who is chosen by the other members.

COUNCIL OF MINISTERS

appointed by the Supreme Soviet. Each minister has department, defense, planning, etc.

SUPREME SOVIET

is the law-making body. It meets twice a year but committees of about 30 of its members meet more regularly to prepare laws. It is made up of two houses: the Council of the Union and the Council of Nationalities.

△ The diagram above illustrates how the CP (Communist Party) dominates the Soviet system.

The CP controls all aspects of government. It chooses who will run the country by appointing the Council of Ministers. Elections are held to choose representatives in the law-making body, the Supreme Soviet. But candidates are chosen by the CP and there is usually only one candidate for each post. This overwhelming control means that the country has been able to make great progress economically in the last 50 years but at great cost: lack of freedom and human rights.

During the 1930s when the modernization plans of the Soviet Union were launched, many objected to the speed of the changes. The Soviet leader, Josef Stalin, used the secret police to "purge" his enemies and all those who opposed the modernization program. Some 32 million citizens were arrested and sent to camps known as *gulags*. It is estimated that some 12 million died.

Gulags exist to this day. It is thought that there are some 4,000 political prisoners out of a total prison population of four million living in the *gulags*. Freedom is severely limited in the communist system but since 1985 the Soviet leader has talked about the need to open up the system for greater "democratization" and individual freedom.

▽ The Soviet newspaper, *Pravda*, is subject to self-censorship, that is, journalists will only write material acceptable to the CP, of which they are members.

Dissidents – the right to protest?

In democratic countries people have the right to object to what the government is doing. They can hold public meetings, set up groups to organize pressure for changes, organize demonstrations and many other forms of protest. The communist system denies people these rights because the interests of the Party come first. In order to push through its programs, the Party imprisons those who oppose it, tortures them and sends them to the *gulags*. Others have been sent to mental hospitals for treatment after being classified as insane. People are not allowed to travel and many of those who want to leave the country, such as Jews, lose their jobs. Newspapers, television and radio are controlled. Letters are intercepted and telephones tapped.

The British government's record on human rights in Northern Ireland is poor. In 1971 members of the security forces were found to have tortured terrorist suspects. The suspects were forced to stand for up to 16 hours with a black hood on their heads. They were denied sleep and food.

Another denial of human rights occurs because the police have wide powers to arrest suspects and hold them for longer than the usual 24 hours.

△ In October 1980 Irish Republican Army terrorists started a "hunger strike" in the Maze Prison in Northern Ireland. They felt they were fighting a war against the British and should be recognized as "political prisoners." This first hunger strike ended before anyone died. A second one was launched in March 1981 and 10 men died before it was called off. The British government refused to make any concessions to the hunger strikers and let them die.

Article 23. (1) Everyone has the right to work, to free choice of employment, to just and favorable conditions of work and to protection against unemployment.

Universal Declaration of Human Rights

Since 1953 critics of the system have become more vocal. These critics are known as "dissidents." The nuclear physicist, Andrey Sakharov, is a leading dissident. He wants to change the communist system so that people can have greater freedom. As he says, "the rights of man have become an absolute necessity." In 1980 he was exiled from Moscow and sent to the town of Gorky but in 1986 he was allowed to return to Moscow to continue his work.

Despite the lack of basic freedoms, most Soviet people accept the Soviet system because it provides their basic needs: food, jobs and housing. In fact, the Soviets point to the millions of unemployed living in poverty in the democratic countries and say this breaches the right to work.

▽ Andrey Sakharov has been fighting for greater freedom in the Soviet Union for the last 20 years. In 1975 the Soviet Union signed the Helsinki Final Acts and agreed to "respect human rights and fundamental freedoms." Sakharov set up a committee to check on the Soviet Union's respect of human rights. Since then he has been persecuted for drawing attention to the Soviet Union's poor record on human rights.

△ The Orgol Special Psychiatric Hospital, where a number of dissidents are supposed to be held. Dissidents are treated with drugs and electric shocks.

Poverty in the Third World

Widespread poverty means that many people cannot enjoy any rights. In the countries of Africa, Asia and South America, often known as the Third World, many people live in poverty.

In 1980 the United Nations commissioned the German politician, Willy Brandt, to look into the problem of poverty. He reported there were 800 million "absolutely poor" on Earth and that the number was rising. A 1986 UN report stated that 12 million children starve to death every year. Brandt also said that one-twentieth of the world's annual military spending would feed and provide services for the poor of the Third World.

▷ A starving woman and child from Ethiopia. Since 1972 Ethiopia has endured several famines, sometimes because of drought and crop failures. In 1972, however, there was enough food to feed everyone but some people were just too poor to buy it.

▽ Slums in Calcutta, India. Although India has succeeded in developing the country, the number of "absolutely poor" has greatly increased.

Universal Declaration of Human Rights

Article 25. (1) Everyone has the right to a standard of living adequate for the health and well-being of himself and of his family, including food, clothing, housing and medical care and necessary social services, and the right to security in the event of unemployment, sickness, disability, widowhood, old age or other lack of livelihood in circumstances beyond his control.

People who can barely survive and are worried about their next meal do not worry about human rights. They do not care whether they can vote or not but are more concerned with getting some form of food and help. Sometimes international relief workers can predict that a famine will occur in countries such as Ethiopia, Somalia and Kampuchea, but nothing is done to prevent it. In fact, Third World countries are often left to cope with their own problems, receiving aid too late and too little. Public response occasionally provides relief, such as Band Aid for Ethiopia, but this is not enough. The problem of poverty has to be solved by the governments of the rich world so that Third World people can enjoy some human rights.

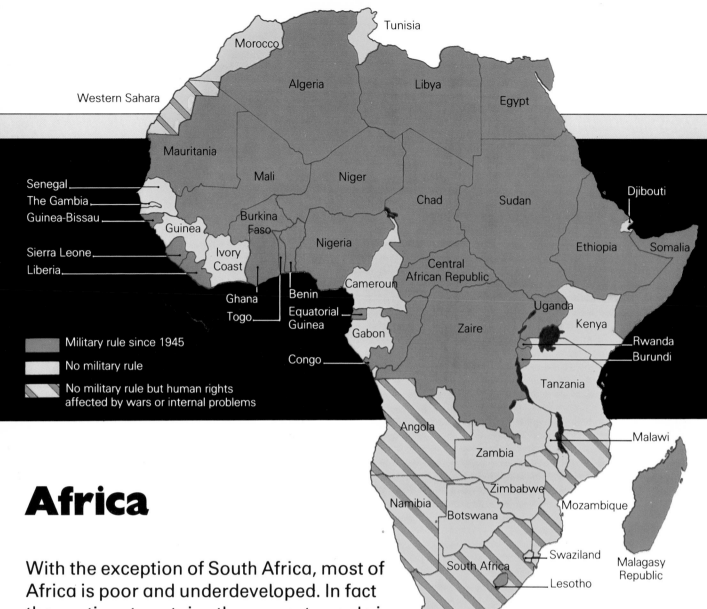

Military rule since 1945

No military rule

No military rule but human rights
affected by wars or internal problems

Africa

With the exception of South Africa, most of
Africa is poor and underdeveloped. In fact
the continent contains the poorest people in
the world. The 23 million Canadians have more
wealth than the 566 million Africans. Many
Africans do not enjoy basic rights.

In Africa a combination of political and
economic problems has led to much unrest,
civil wars and wars between countries. During
wartime many countries do not allow their
people rights. People are not allowed out at
night, soldiers kill innocent people, newspapers
are not allowed to report what is happening and
other measures are taken. Sometimes the army
decides that its leaders would make a better job
of running their country than the political leaders
and they stage a coup. Since 1945 there have
been more than 60 successful coups in Africa.

△ This map shows the
number of countries under
military rule in Africa.
In the past some have
experienced brutal
governments whose soldiers
have killed thousands of
people. For example, in
Uganda some 750,000 people
died during the military regime
of General Idi Amin (1971-79).

△ In 1981 an army council seized power in Ghana. The photograph shows a political rally being held by the government to increase its support.

Once in power, the military leaders do not respect human rights. Some military rulers have become notorious for their cruelty. For example, President Macias Nguema of Equatorial Guinea is thought to have been responsible for 43,000 deaths out of a population of 350,000. In 1985 the communist leader of Ethiopia, General Mengistu Haile Mariam, added to the problems of his country by the forced resettlement of 1.5 million people. He claimed this was for their own good to protect them from famine. In fact, he wanted to make sure they did not help his opponents and many died as a result.

Some countries, notably Senegal and Botswana, have avoided military rule and have good records on human rights. This is because they have avoided war and unrest despite the great poverty of their people.

△ General Mengistu of Ethiopia came to power in a military coup in 1974. Faced with a war against Somalia, rebels in Eritrea and famine, human rights have suffered in Ethiopia.

South Africa-apartheid state

South Africa is singled out for its human rights record because of apartheid – the set of laws that keep the white minority in power over the majority black people. In 1950 the white government passed the Group Areas Act that deprived most blacks of human rights by only allowing them to live in certain territories (Bantustans). These comprise 13 per cent of the land for 23 million blacks. Most of the land is allocated to the 4.5 million whites.

Black people live on the poorest land in appalling conditions. There is no work in the Bantustans. Blacks *can* work in the white areas but they have to live in the special settlements or townships, such as Soweto. They cannot live with their families, who have to live in the Bantustans. Until recently the apartheid system covered all aspects of life, for example, there were separate buses for whites and blacks.

▽ A woman picks through debris at the Crossroads "squatter" settlement near Cape Town, 1986. The squatters are usually wives and children of black workers. By law they have no right to be there. So the police and army move in to bulldoze the settlements and force the people back to their "homelands." However, they usually return to build a new home.

Since 1976 black violence has been on the increase and many have been killed in anti-apartheid protests. South Africa has the most notorious secret police in the world. Many black leaders have died while being held by the police, and torture is often used during interrogation.

Under pressure from the democratic countries of North America and Western Europe, the South African governments has started to reform apartheid by giving greater rights to Indian and Colored (mixed) people, but blacks still do not have any political rights. This led to more unrest and rioting in the townships increased. In 1986 the government declared a state of emergency and suspended many human rights. Newspapers and television crews are not allowed to report what is going on. Public meetings cannot be held without permission of the police. This is likely to continue for some time.

△ The symbol of the Anti-Apartheid Movement of Great Britain. It exists to put pressure on the British government not to support South Africa's apartheid system.

▽ Whites look on at a black on "their" bus. The recent reforms of apartheid mean that blacks and whites can travel on the same bus. But it will take years before whites accept this as normal.

Central and South America

Central and South America are full of extremes: most of the wealth is in the hands of a few of the descendants of the European colonizers; the rest including the indigenous Indian and other minorities live in poverty. Brazil is the most rapidly developing country yet the gap between rich and poor is getting worse – not better. No one can enjoy social rights in the slums of the larger cities, such as Rio de Janeiro.

In terms of civil and political rights, South America also has a bad human rights record. It has a history of dictators (often a general) kept in power by the army. Argentina, Peru, Chile, Paraguay, Bolivia, Brazil, El Salvador and Guatemala have all had extremely brutal military rulers. From 1976-83 Argentina had a military government. Some 24,000 people are thought to be "missing," including 400 children and 1,000 pregnant women. When democracy was restored not many were found.

▷ Until 1983 Argentina was ruled by a military government. Every Thursday at 3:30 p.m. the mothers and grandmothers of those who had disappeared silently walked around the Plaza de Mayos in Buenos Aires. This was their protest against disappearances and it has brought worldwide attention to the brutality of the military government. Even after the restoration of democracy the mothers and grandmothers continued to demonstrate.

Commovedor documento

LOS NIÑOS DESAPARECIDOS

◁ During 1981 and 1982 El Salvador was the focus of world attention because of its death squads. Victims included children, nuns, priests, medical workers and many others. In this photograph the bodies of two pregnant women, a girl and two men have been discovered on the outskirts of San Salvador, March 1981.

In Central America the most sinister human rights abuse are the death squads. Made up of soldiers and policemen, the death squads patrol the streets at night and arrest government opponents, leaving their bodies to be discovered on the roadsides. Anyone who criticizes the government can be at the mercy of the death squads, for example, writers, musicians and artists. In the 1980s death squads have appeared in other Central and South American countries.

Southeast Asia

Southeast Asia is one of the most densely populated parts of the world. In order to govern such a mass of people, human rights have been ignored. In Kampuchea the communist Khmer Rouge came to power in 1975. They wanted to change society completely and to build a new communist system. In the process of achieving this they jailed huge numbers of people. They also sent millions out of the cities to live in the countryside, where they were to be "re-educated." Nearly a third – 1.4 million – of the Kampuchean people died.

In 1979 neighboring Vietnam, also communist, invaded Kampuchea to throw out the Khmer Rouge, who went into the jungle to fight the invaders. In the chaos, millions were near starvation and famine was only avoided with aid from the United States and Europe.

Vietnam also became involved in war with China in 1979. Within Vietnam there was a sizable Chinese minority, which was subjected to mass arrrests, enslavement in camps and executions. Rather than face this, the Chinese minority chose to escape by sea in junks. These people were known as "Boat People" and many died trying to escape Vietnam. Some Vietnamese also fled their country to escape the communist government. Many of these refugees were picked up by ships and taken to nearby ports, where they waited to be resettled in North America, Europe or the Far East.

In order to continue the occupation of Kampuchea, Vietnam has the third largest army in the world. This puts an enormous strain on the country's economy and further worsens the conditions in which the people live. In Kampuchea the continuing guerrilla war extends to Thailand and threatens human rights there.

△ Boat People being picked out of the South China Sea by a German ship. When the refugees left Vietnam they took very little with them. Some took gold in the hope of starting a new life somewhere else, but most were so desperate to leave the country that was persecuting them that they left all their possessions behind in Vietnam.

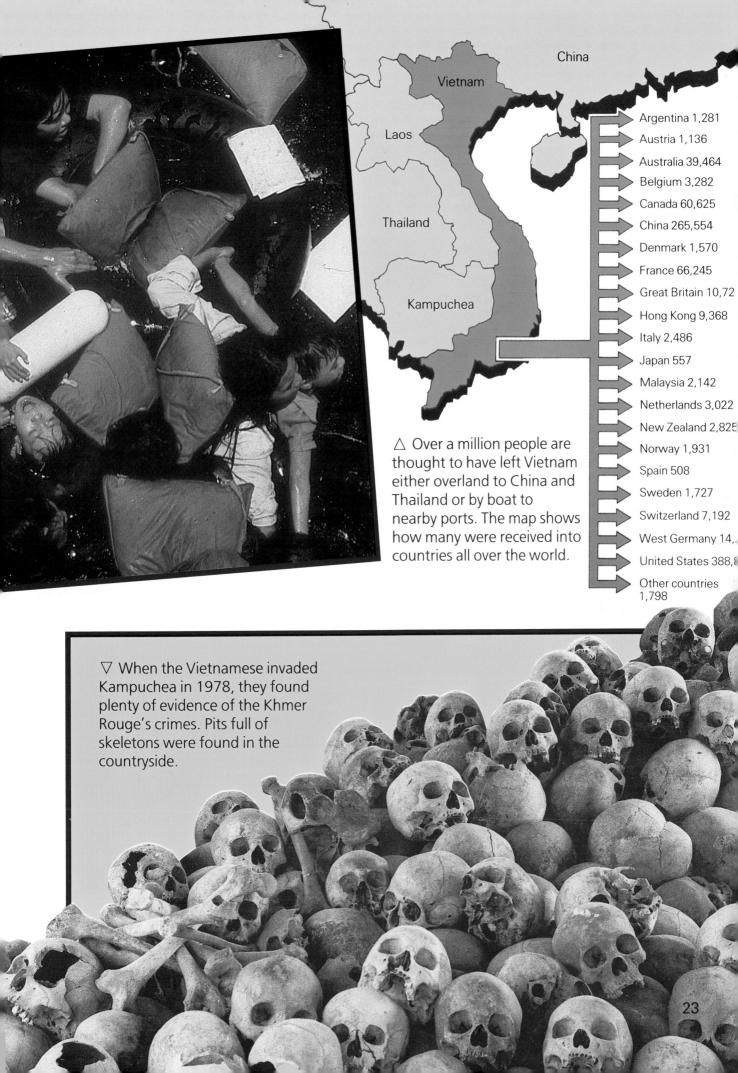

Argentina 1,281
Austria 1,136
Australia 39,464
Belgium 3,282
Canada 60,625
China 265,554
Denmark 1,570
France 66,245
Great Britain 10,72
Hong Kong 9,368
Italy 2,486
Japan 557
Malaysia 2,142
Netherlands 3,022
New Zealand 2,825
Norway 1,931
Spain 508
Sweden 1,727
Switzerland 7,192
West Germany 14,
United States 388,8
Other countries 1,798

△ Over a million people are thought to have left Vietnam either overland to China and Thailand or by boat to nearby ports. The map shows how many were received into countries all over the world.

▽ When the Vietnamese invaded Kampuchea in 1978, they found plenty of evidence of the Khmer Rouge's crimes. Pits full of skeletons were found in the countryside.

23

The Muslim World

▽ Under Islamic law women are expected to care for the family and stay at home. Some Islamic countries in the Middle East allow women to work outside the home. In Iran, however, women must follow Islamic law. They are not allowed to reveal their bodies and can only leave the house if they are wearing the correct clothes.

The Muslim World covers the Middle East, North Africa, Malaysia, Indonesia, Pakistan, Bangladesh and is spreading worldwide. Most Muslim countries are subject to Islamic or Shari'a law, which goes against the West's ideas about human rights. All ideas hostile to Islam are banned. Those who reject Islam lose their life. Drinking alcohol is punishable by flogging. Theft is punished by cutting off a hand. Men can marry as many as four wives and divorce any they do not like. Women have very few rights and cannot even travel on their own.

Some countries, such as Saudi Arabia, have indicated that they might reform their laws. However, Islamic fundamentalists totally reject the West's view on human rights.

△ A Sudanese association for those who have lost their hands following punishment by Islamic law. They have joined together to help each other cope.

In Iran, where Shi'ite fundamentalists are in power, Islamic law is applied severely. Thousands are held in prisons without trial. Trials only last a few minutes and at least eight people were stoned to death in 1986. Children as young as 11 were executed in 1981. Floggings are common and an unmarried couple who kiss can receive up to 99 lashes.

People in democratic countries find this kind of punishment outrageous. But Shi'ite fundamentalists find many of the habits and customs of democratic countries intolerable. They consider that women in the West have too much freedom outside the home. It is very unlikely that the Muslim World and the West will ever agree on human rights.

▽ Women and children celebrate the coming to power of the Shi'ite fundamentalists in Iran. Under Islamic law children undergo Islamic education and are not allowed any other religious teaching. In the West this is seen as "brainwashing" and is unacceptable.

Defending human rights

Since 1945 many organizations have been set up to ensure the protection of human rights. The United Nations has no power to make sure that its members observe the Universal Declaration of Human Rights but it has many specialized agencies to deal with specific problems. For example, the United Nation's Development Program encourages richer countries to put money into Third World development projects. The Food and Agriculture Organization tries to improve farming and fishing methods worldwide. The United Nation's Children's Fund (UNICEF) helps children in poorer countries.

Other international organizations exist to defend human rights. The Organization of American States takes up cases of human rights abuses in North and South America and tries to put pressure on countries to improve their record. In Europe anyone can bring a complaint before the European Court of Human Rights, which hears 400 cases every year.

The best defense of human rights is pressure from people and newspapers, television and radio. Amnesty International is a pressure group that draws the world's attention to human rights abuses. It publishes regular reports on political prisoners, torture, slavery and other abuses. By alerting people to particular cases it can get some people released from jail. Other groups exist to defend particular human rights issues. For example, the National Council for Civil Liberties tries to ensure civil and political rights in Great Britain are respected.

Useful addresses:
Amnesty International
UN Office
777 United Nations Plaza
New York, NY 100117
(212) 867-8878

Center of Concern (Human Rights)
3700 13th Street, NE
Washington, DC 20017
(202) 635-2757

Center for International Policy (Human Rights)
120 Maryland Avenue, NE
Washington, DC 20002

International League for Human Rights
432 Park Avenue South
New York, NY 10016
(212) 684-1221

▷ The symbol of Amnesty International which was set up in 1961 to fight for human rights worldwide.

△ Romeo Castillo is released from prison in the Philippines. He was adopted by an Amnesty International group as a "prisoner of conscience." They wrote letters asking for his release to important people in his country and raised his case in their own country.

Extending freedom worldwide

Human rights are a worldwide problem. Countries that do not respect human rights cannot be forced to put them into practice but they can be pressurized by other countries. The United Nations exists to provide a forum for debate. If a particular country is not respecting human rights then this can be raised there. The United Nations is also drawing up a treaty which would make torture an international crime.

Recently the superpowers (the United States and the Soviet Union) have been showing a greater concern for human rights. The United States is more reluctant to give aid to countries that have a bad human rights record, although it still supports the government of El Salvador.

However, the best way of extending freedom is to create a demand for it among the people. This happened recently in the Philippines. In 1986 President Ferdinand Marcos won the elections. However following evidence of electoral fraud, people protested and Marcos left the country.

▽ Ex-President Ferdinand Marcos (left) and President Corazon Aquino (right). It is not always possible to guarantee human rights in a democratic country. Many argued that Marcos stayed in power because he rigged elections. Aquino came to power in the Philippines in 1986 because the people had had enough of the corrupt rule of Marcos. She has faced many problems in trying to extend freedom in her country, namely a guerrilla war with the communists and the threat of a military takeover. In 1987, however, she won a massive victory in the elections.

The Soviet Union has come under a lot of pressure to improve its human rights record. Every time a Western leader visits Moscow the issue is raised. At the arms control negotiations human rights have also been raised. In fact, the Soviet Union has recently released prisoners and allowed more Jews to leave the country. However, the Soviets have only released some 300 dissidents.

Although changes in the Soviet system may take years to come into effect, there is evidence that General Secretary Mikhail Gorbachev is succeeding in introducing greater openness or *glasnost* into the Soviet system. He has gotten rid of many of the "old" party leaders who were corrupt and would have stopped any changes. These are encouraging signs for the future.

However, in order to extend human rights worldwide the rich world must tackle the problem of poverty. There are few signs that this will happen in the next few years.

▽ General Secretary Mikhail Gorbachev talks to factory workers. Gorbachev believes the Soviet system must be able to absorb criticism. He is willing to talk to people and hear their complaints. The previous leadership never came into contact with the people. This is part of the *glasnost* which he is advocating. Newspapers and television have been allowed greater freedom to criticize the communist system. There are regular programs on television where people are asked to raise problems with government ministers. This has led to many lively exchanges.

Hard facts

Women's Rights

Women make up half the world's population but they often suffer discrimination and lack of many human rights.

In 1979 the Convention on the Elimination of All Forms of Discrimination against Women was adopted by the United Nations to try to improve conditions for women. However, only a third of the members of the United Nations have signed it.

In any case it is very difficult to overcome discrimination against women. Equal Pay Acts and Anti-Discrimination laws do not change things overnight. Many women still get low pay the world over.

Another aspect of women's inequality is that men dominate governments. There have been rare exceptions such as Margaret Thatcher of Great Britain, Indira Gandhi of India and Corazon Aquino of the Philippines. In the English-speaking democracies only up to 10 per cent of elected representatives are women. Equality for women is a long way from being achieved.

▷ All the information for this map is taken from *The Economist World Human Rights Guide*, published in 1986. It estimates that only one person in five enjoys human rights. Below are some examples of abuses of human rights:

Chile
Since 1973, when the military came to power, human rights have been under threat. In 1984 the police were reported to have injured 500 and killed 50 suspects after arrest.

Africa
Most of the countries that do not respect human rights in Africa do not allow any opposition to the government, which is often backed by the army. Travel is restricted and the government controls newspapers, television and radio. Most women do not have equal rights.

Soviet Union and its allies
The Soviet Union, Eastern Europe, Cuba, Mozambique, Ethiopia, Angola, Vietnam, Laos and Afghanistan all have a communist sytem of government. This means no opposition is allowed. There are labor camps for government opponents. Newspapers, television and radio are controlled. Travel is restricted. However women do have equal opportunities.

The Muslim World
In the Muslim World opposition to Islam is not allowed and other religions are persecuted. The enforcement of Shari'a law varies from country to country. Newspapers, television and radio are controlled. Women do not have equal rights. Sometimes women have been stoned for adultery. The Kurdish minority in Iran, Syria and Turkey is persecuted.

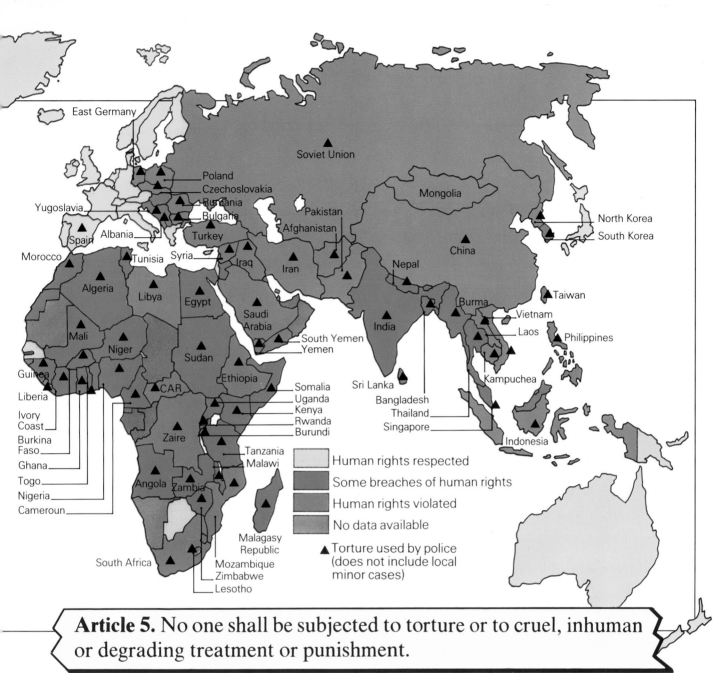

East Germany
Soviet Union
Poland
Czechoslovakia
Rumania
Bulgaria
Yugoslavia
Spain
Albania
Turkey
Morocco
Tunisia
Syria
Iraq
Pakistan
Afghanistan
Mongolia
North Korea
South Korea
China
Algeria
Libya
Egypt
Iran
Nepal
Taiwan
Saudi Arabia
Burma
Vietnam
Laos
Mali
Niger
Sudan
South Yemen
Yemen
India
Philippines
Guinea
CAR
Ethiopia
Sri Lanka
Kampuchea
Liberia
Somalia
Bangladesh
Ivory Coast
Zaire
Uganda
Kenya
Thailand
Burkina Faso
Rwanda
Singapore
Ghana
Burundi
Indonesia
Togo
Tanzania
Nigeria
Malawi
Cameroun
Angola
Zambia

Human rights respected
Some breaches of human rights
Human rights violated
No data available
▲ Torture used by police (does not include local minor cases)

Malagasy Republic
South Africa
Mozambique
Zimbabwe
Lesotho

Article 5. No one shall be subjected to torture or to cruel, inhuman or degrading treatment or punishment.

Universal Declaration of Human Rights

China
China is a communist country but is not allied to the Soviet Union. However its people suffer similar loss of rights as in other communist countries. In 1986 some 5,000 people were executed for various crimes including theft, sometimes by shooting in the neck. If a couple have more than one child they are penalized. Travel is controlled.

Indonesia
Indonesia is a Muslim country. The people in Loro Sae and Irian Jaya are virtually enslaved. The Chinese minority is discriminated against. Women do not have equal rights.

Israel and Palestine
Those Palestinians living in Israel are treated as second class citizens and are subject to discrimination.

Torture
Torture has been practiced for centuries. Methods of torture have become increasingly sophisticated, for example, drugs and electric shocks are used. However the most common forms of torture are burning with cigarettes, being tied up, lack of sleep and food and near drowning.

Index

Photographic Credits:
Cover and pages 13 (left), 21, 24 (right) and
27: Amnesty International; page 5: Edwin
Tulalian/Amnesty International; pages 8, 9, 10,
13 (right), 28 (both) and back cover: Rex
Features; page 12: Topham; pages 14-15, 22-
23 and 23: Stern; page 15: B. Campbell/
UNICEF/Amnesty International; page 17 (top):
Hutchison Library; page 17 (bottom):
Photosource; pages 18, 24 (left), 25 and 29:
Frank Spooner Agency; page 19: Popperfoto;
page 20: Chris Steele-Perkins/Hillelson Agency.